# Moder
# Metro....

D0106058

**Artist's Images of
New York**

**23 Postcards
from the
Museum of
the City
of New York**

**Edited by
Leslie Nolan**

This selection of twenty-three prints, from more than 10,000 in the collection of the Museum of the City of New York, spans New York City's architectural renewal, from the first decade of the twentieth century through the onslaught of the Depression, and shows many dimensions of urban life—the dynamic architectural landscape, pedestrians and street traffic, the prosperous and destitute. All of these became common subject matter in prints during this period. Indeed, never before or since have so many printmakers captured New York City's energetic rhythms in such an array of styles.

These prints also reflect their makers' experimentation with new or newly revived printmaking media. The woodcut, linoleum cut, lithograph, and silkscreen had previously been used primarily in commercial illustration. Now these techniques were employed in the pursuit of more ambitious artistic goals. But it was New York's arresting subject matter, too, that helped elevate the print medium to a higher standing, achieving new prominence for the "democratic art." No subject was too daunting or too "low": the sweep of towering skyscrapers, the labyrinth of buried subways, revelers at the beach, dancers cheek to cheek, backstage theater, or frenetic workers. Many of these artists must have taken to heart Reginald Marsh's advice: "Go out into the street, stare at the people. Go into the subway. Stare at the people. Stare, stare, keep on staring."

The prints in this book were made between 1910 and 1940. Those made for the New York City Graphics Division of the Works Progress (later "Work Projects") Administration (1935-1943) are particularly compelling. The WPA was responsible for advances in printmaking technology and their dissemination. The New York City Graphics Division of the WPA employed hundreds of artists and reaped a harvest of more than 200,000 impressions of 11,000 images. The WPA prints are notable for their attention to the commonplace and to the strife of daily life. But all of these prints frame the new and the familiar in striking, modernist compositions.

Leslie Nolan
Curator, Prints and Photographs
Museum of the City of New York

**Queensboro Bridge**, 1930, Louis Lozowick (1892-1973)
Lithograph, Edition 50, Museum of the City of New York
Purchase, 84.94.4

In 1927 Lozowick wrote: "The dominant trend in America today, beneath all the apparent chaos and confusion. . .is toward order and organization which find their outward. . .symbol in the rigid geometry of the American city: in the verticals of the smokestacks, in the parallels of its car tracks and the squares of its streets, the cubes of its factories, the arc of its bridges, the cylinders of its gas tanks."  The sparsely populated borough of Queens voted in 1898 to become part of Greater New York on the promise of easier access to Manhattan. In 1909 the Queensboro Bridge, one of the first bridge spans to be designed by both an engineer and an architect—Henry Hornbostel—replaced ferries as the means of cross-river transport.

MODERN METROPOLIS © The Museum of the City of New York
1993 The New Press

**Garment District**, 1934, Don Freeman (1908-1978)
Lithograph, Edition 50, Museum of the City of New York
Permanent Deposit of the Whitney Museum of American Art, 1226.11

Originally concentrated on the Lower East Side late in the nineteenth
century, by the 1930s the garment center moved northward and westward to
the middle of Manhattan between Sixth and Ninth Avenues, from Thirtieth
to Forty-second Streets. By the 1930s, three out of four American ready-made
coats and dresses were produced there. Freeman's ebullient scenes center
on the fortitude and humor of urbanites rather than the hopelessness and
despair portrayed by other artists.

MODERN METROPOLIS © The Museum of the City of New York
1993 The New Press

**Brother Can You Spare a Dime?**, c. 1930, Albert Potter (1903-1937)
Linoleum cut, Museum of the City of New York
Gift of Mr. Irving Potter, 87.62.4

An unemployed man dominates a background of symbols of New York's
dynamism: crowds pouring into subways, a montage of shop signs, and well-
known skyscrapers. Above it all, the figure of death presides. With the onset
of the Great Depression, over one-third of the city's work force found itself
unemployed. Faced with an accelerating national jobless rate, thousands of
laid-off wage earners migrated to New York City, only to have their expecta-
tions of finding work soon dashed. Some managed to eke out an existence
by selling apples, pencils, and flowers on the streets; others went on
government relief; many wound up as vagrants relying on breadlines and
park bench sleeping berths.

MODERN METROPOLIS © The Museum of the City of New York
1993 The New Press

**Washington's Birthday Parade, Fifth Avenue & 23rd**, 1916
Childe Hassam (1859-1935)
Etching, Museum of the City of New York
Gift of Mr. Storrs Haynes, 58.333

The Fuller Building, designed by Daniel H. Burnham and Company (1903),
popularly known as the Flatiron Building, was singularly celebrated in the
fledgling skyscraper era. The building's flatiron shape filled the small,
triangular plot at the intersection of Broadway and Twenty-third Street.
The building, which captured the imaginations of countless artists, quickly
emerged as an icon of modern Manhattan.

first
class
postage
here

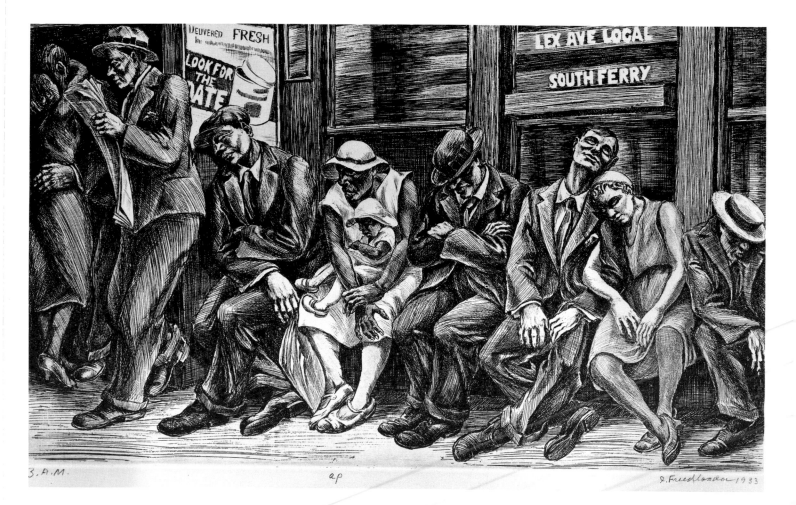

3.A.M.                                                                    ap                                                    I. Freedlander 1933

**3 A.M.**, 1933, Isac Friedlander (1890-1968)
Etching, Museum of the City of New York
Gift of Mrs. Isac Friedlander, 82.20

Born in Russia, Friedlander spent six years in prison for anticzarist political
activities before traveling to Europe and finally settling in the United States
in 1929. Urbanites depended on the twenty-four-hour interborough subway
service, reinforcing New York's image as the "city that never sleeps."

MODERN METROPOLIS © The Museum of the City of New York
1993 The New Press

**Evening in Central Park**, 1923, Jan Matulka (1890-1972)
Lithograph, Museum of the City of New York, Purchase, 83.111

Matulka was born in Czechoslovakia.  Boating on the lake in Central Park
had become so popular by the late nineteenth century that the Department
of Parks decided to construct a boathouse to accommodate the droves of
"Sunday sailors" who found the existing landing at the Terrace Esplanade
inadequate.

first
class
postage
here

Hot Summer Night

**One Summer Night**, c. 1936-1942, Saul Kovner (b. 1904)
Lithograph, Edition 25, Museum of the City of New York
Gift of Work Projects Administration, 43.129.27

Born in Russia, Kovner exhibited at the 1939 World's Fair in Queens.
Kovner was able to create the sense of oppressive heat that descends on
New York in the summertime. While well-to-do New Yorkers were able to
escape to the mountains or the beach, these tenement dwellers sought relief
from the city's heat on their own roof-top "tar beach."

MODERN METROPOLIS © The Museum of the City of New York
1993 The New Press

COFFEE POT

**First Avenue Market**, 1934, Louis Lozowick (1892-1973)
Lithograph, Edition 10, Museum of the City of New York
Permanent Deposit of the Whitney Museum of American Art, 1226.4

This print was commissioned by the Public Works of Art Program (PWAP)
from which Lozowick received approval for a series of prints on the New York
urban scene showing life and labor in various districts of the city.

MODERN METROPOLIS © The Museum of the City of New York
1993 The New Press

**Coney Island Beach**, 1935, Reginald Marsh (1898-1954)
Etching, Edition 24; American Artists Group Edition 200
Museum of the City of New York, Purchase, 83.154.2

Marsh's fascination with the "crowds of people in all directions, in all
positions," led him repeatedly to those few miles of sand and boardwalk
at the southern tip of Brooklyn.

first
class
postage
here

**Organizational Advances**, c. 1930, Albert Potter (1903-1937)
Linoleum cut, Museum of the City of New York
Gift of Mr. Irving Potter, 87.62.5

Potter's concern for the plight of the common man during the Great
Depression is evident as a group of men—surrounded by the El and
towering buildings—wear advertising placards and are overshadowed
by a skeleton promulgating "vitality."

MODERN METROPOLIS © The Museum of the City of New York
1993 The New Press

**Bar**, 1929, Joseph Golinkin (1896-1977)
Lithograph, Museum of the City of New York
Gift of Mr. James M. Holzman, 57.176.2

With the 1933 repeal of the Eighteenth Amendment to the U.S. Constitution, which outlawed the consumption of intoxicants, bars and clubs serving liquor were once again legal in the United States. But at the time Golinkin created this suave scene, Prohibition was in effect.

first
class
postage
here

The Savoy

Dugford Bransfield

**The Savoy**, c.1936-1942, Dayton Brandfield
Lithograph, Edition 25, Museum of the City of New York
Gift of Work Projects Administration, 43.129.3

Born in Utah, Brandfield studied in Paris before moving to West 81st Street
in Manhattan. Harlem's best-known dance hall during the Great Depression
was the Savoy Ballroom, located at Lenox Avenue and 140th Street. Dances
originating at the Savoy include the Lindy Hop, Truckin', The Susie Q, and
the Shag. Chick Webb, Duke Ellington, Louis Armstrong, and Ella Fitzgerald
were among the luminaries who performed there.

MODERN METROPOLIS © The Museum of the City of New York
1993 The New Press

**Gas House**, c.1936-1942, Harold Anchel (1912-1980)
Lithograph, Edition 25, Museum of the City of New York
Gift of Work Projects Administration, 43.129.1

Anchel worked for the Civil Works Administration for Federal Buildings in
Manhattan.  He exhibited with other WPA artists at the Federal Art Project
Gallery located at 225 West 57th Street in Manhattan. The "gas house district"
stretched from the East River to Third Avenue from 14th to 27th Streets.

MODERN METROPOLIS © The Museum of the City of New York
1993 The New Press

**Burlycue**, 1936, Kyra Markham (1891-1967)
Lithograph, Edition 25, Museum of the City of New York
Gift of Work Projects Administration, 43.129.37

In order to support her career as an actress, Markham made bookjacket
illustrations, before turning to the creation of murals in powder rooms,
restaurants, and bars. By 1934 she had taken up lithography, and may
have worked backstage for George and Ira Gershwin's 1935 production
of "Porgy and Bess."

MODERN METROPOLIS © The Museum of the City of New York
1993 The New Press

**Coney Island**, 1932, Isac Friedlander (1890-1968)
Aquatint, Museum of the City of New York
Gift of Mrs. Isac Friedlander, 82.25.2

Born in Russia, Friedlander spent six years in prison for anticzarist political
activities before traveling to Europe and finally settling in the United States in
1929. Coney Island, an island only in name, has provided New Yorkers with
summer recreation and respite from the city's sweltering heat for almost two
centuries.  Its first resort hotel, Coney Island House, was built in 1829. With
the introduction of rides and other boardwalk attractions in the late nineteenth
century, Coney Island blossomed into a vast seaside amusement park. By 1905,
its diversions included the famous roller coaster Cyclone, unveiled in 1884, the
Ferris Wheel, the brilliantly illuminated Luna Park, and Dreamland.

MODERN METROPOLIS © The Museum of the City of New York
1993 The New Press

**Backstage "Porgy and Bess,"** 1936, Kyra Markham (1891-1967)
Lithograph, Edition 25, Museum of the City of New York
Gift of Work Projects Administration, 43.129.40

In order to support her career as an actress, Markham made bookjacket
illustrations, before turning to the creation of murals in powder rooms,
restaurants, and bars. By 1934 she had taken up lithography and may
have worked backstage for George and Ira Gershwin's 1935 production
of "Porgy and Bess."

MODERN METROPOLIS © The Museum of the City of New York
1993 The New Press

**Red Hots**, c.1936-1942, Carlos Anderson (b. 1905)
Lithograph, Edition 25, Museum of the City of New York
Gift of Work Projects Administration, 43.129.4

In 1936, New York's hotdog vendors, along with other pushcart peddlers, numbered nearly 14,000—almost equal to the number of police in the city. The city's Department of Markets sought to eliminate "curb carts," and the health commissioner along with Mayor LaGuardia argued for a policy that would ban them. A common fear was that street peddlers would throw thousands of hard-working retail shopkeepers onto home relief. In 1938, a ban on pushcart peddlers went into effect, and municipal markets were established under one roof.

first
class
postage
here

**The Bridge**, c. 1930, Albert Potter (1903-1937)
Linoleum cut, Museum of the City of New York
Gift of Mr. Irving Potter, 87.62.2

Spanning New York's East River, the Brooklyn Bridge (1867-1883), designed
by John A. and Washington Roebling, was the longest suspension bridge in
the world. Historian Lewis Mumford wrote of this engineering triumph: "All
that the age had just cause for pride in—its advances in science, its skill in
handling iron, its personal heroism in the face of dangerous industrial
processes, its willingness to attempt the untried and the impossible—came
to a head in Brooklyn Bridge."

MODERN METROPOLIS © The Museum of the City of New York
1993 The New Press

**L'Art Moderne**, c. 1936-1942, Joseph Golinkin (1896-1977)
Lithograph, Museum of the City of New York, Purchase, 86.36

The 1913 Armory Show in New York City was a beachhead for avant-garde
European styles. Its effects were increasingly apparent as galleries and
museums exhibited what progressive critics lauded as "the New Art."

first
class
postage
here

**Subway**, 1934, Fritz Eichenberg (German born, 1901-1990)
Woodcut, Museum of the City of New York
Gift of Mrs. Constance Veit Sherwin, 62.160.8

Eichenberg: "Since its origin the woodblock has been the most democratic
medium in art.  Whatever its social, political, or religious significance may
have been, it has always been the carrier of a message."  When plans for the
first Interborough Rapid Transit (IRT) subway line (from City Hall to West
145th Street) were announced in 1900, Russell Sage remarked: "New York
people will never go into a hole in the ground to ride. . . .Preposterous!" By
the 1930s about 5,500,000 passengers commuted daily on the New York City
subway system.

first
class
postage
here

**Late Editions**, 1934, Don Freeman (1908-1978)
Lithograph, Edition 10, Museum of the City of New York
Permanent Deposit of the Whitney Museum of American Art, 1226.14

Describing his New York City images, Freeman asserted: "I had to keep
drawing so as to let the world know what wonderful people I had come
across—not only the way they looked, but the way they invented lives for
themselves out of nothing: carrying signs, fishing for change through side-
walk gratings, shining shoes, peddling gardenias, selling corsets, plugging
song hits, washing windows, sharpening knives."

MODERN METROPOLIS © The Museum of the City of New York
1993 The New Press

**Old Aquarium**, 1936, Mabel Dwight (1876-1955)
Lithograph, Edition 25, Museum of the City of New York
Gift of Work Projects Administration, 43.129.12

Set in Battery Park, the Aquarium was a circular, three-story building,
originally constructed as a harbor fort known as the West Battery in 1807,
and renamed Castle Clinton after the War of 1812. When its military
function was no longer necessary, the structure was ceded to the city as
Castle Garden and became the scene of notable public and social events,
one of which was Jenny Lind's American concert debut in 1850. In 1855,
Castle Garden became the country's chief station of immigration. In 1890,
Ellis Island took over as an immigrant reception center, and Castle Garden
was closed, to be opened six years later as the Aquarium of the City of
New York. The building shell is still there today—known as Castle Clinton—
but the aquarium was closed in 1942.

**Civic Insomnia**, 1932, Gerald Geerlings (b. 1897)
Aquatint, Edition 38, Museum of the City of New York
Gift of Mr. Allen Townsend Terrell, 70.63.7

Trained as an architect at the University of Pennsylvania, Geerling's predominant graphic interests were the constructed environment of American cities. Here, rich tonal gradations and surface texture shroud the New York City skyline.

first
class
postage
here